Table of Contents

Chapter 1: Introduction to XRP

What is XRP?

XRP is a digital asset created by Ripple Labs, designed primarily for facilitating cross-border payments. Unlike traditional cryptocurrencies like Bitcoin, which aim to serve as a medium of exchange, XRP focuses on providing liquidity and enabling faster, cheaper transactions across different currencies. Launched in 2012, XRP operates on a unique consensus algorithm that allows for rapid transaction processing, making it an attractive option for financial institutions looking to optimize their payment systems. This efficiency is key to understanding XRP's role in the evolving landscape of digital finance.

One of the most significant advantages of XRP is its ability to settle transactions in just a few seconds. This speed is particularly beneficial in the context of international payments, where traditional methods can take days to process. By using XRP as a bridge currency, financial institutions can significantly reduce the time and cost associated with cross-border transactions. This capability places XRP at the forefront of discussions regarding the future of global payments, as it addresses many of the pain points associated with legacy systems.

When comparing XRP to other cryptocurrencies, it is essential to highlight its unique positioning. Many cryptocurrencies emphasize decentralization and serve as investment vehicles or stores of value. In contrast, XRP was designed with a specific utility in mind — facilitating remittances and enhancing liquidity for banks and payment providers. This focus on practicality and real-world use cases differentiates XRP from alternatives like Ethereum or Bitcoin, which have broader applications beyond payments. Understanding these distinctions is crucial for anyone interested in how various cryptocurrencies can serve different market needs.

The technology behind XRP is equally important to grasp. XRP operates on an open-source ledger known as the XRP Ledger, which utilizes a consensus protocol rather than the mining processes found in Bitcoin and other cryptocurrencies. This design choice allows for faster transactions and lower energy consumption. The XRP Ledger also supports smart contracts, enabling developers to build applications on top of it. This technological foundation not only enhances XRP's efficiency but also positions it as a viable option for integration into existing financial infrastructures.

XRP's partnerships with financial institutions further underscore its potential in the modern financial landscape. Ripple has formed alliances with numerous banks and payment providers worldwide, enabling them to leverage XRP for their payment solutions. These collaborations highlight the asset's utility and facilitate its integration into traditional finance. Additionally, as decentralized finance (DeFi) continues to gain traction, XRP's role may evolve, potentially contributing to innovative financial products and services that bridge the gap between traditional banking and emerging digital finance solutions. Understanding these dynamics is essential for anyone looking to navigate the complexities of cryptocurrency and its implications for the future of finance.

Brief History of Ripple and XRP

Ripple was founded in 2012 by Chris Larsen and Jed McCaleb, initially as a technology company focused on developing real-time gross settlement systems. The vision behind Ripple was to create a network that could facilitate instant, low-cost international money transfers, addressing the inefficiencies prevalent in traditional banking systems. The company initially launched RipplePay, which allowed users to send money across borders using any currency. This innovation laid the groundwork for what would eventually become Ripple's more advanced protocols and the introduction of its native digital asset, XRP.

XRP was created as a bridge currency to enhance the functionality of the Ripple network. Unlike Bitcoin and many other cryptocurrencies, which aim to be a store of value or a medium of exchange, XRP was specifically designed for use in cross-border payments. Utilizing the Ripple protocol, XRP can be used to facilitate transactions between different fiat currencies, providing liquidity and reducing the need for pre-funded accounts in destination currencies. This unique positioning has made XRP an attractive option for financial institutions seeking to streamline their cross-border payment processes.

Over the years, Ripple has formed numerous partnerships with banks and financial institutions worldwide, showcasing the practical applications of XRP in real-world scenarios. Institutions like Santander and American Express have explored integrating Ripple's technology to improve their payment systems. These partnerships have demonstrated the potential of XRP as a solution for real-time settlement and liquidity management, significantly enhancing the speed and efficiency of transactions compared to traditional methods that often take days to process.

In addition to its role in cross-border payments, XRP has garnered attention in the burgeoning field of decentralized finance (DeFi). While Ripple itself is not a decentralized platform in the same way as Ethereum, the growing interest in DeFi has spurred discussions about how XRP can fit into this ecosystem. Some projects are exploring the use of XRP for lending, borrowing, and other financial services, which could expand its utility beyond just payments. This evolving landscape presents both challenges and opportunities for XRP as it seeks to maintain relevance in a rapidly changing financial environment.

Despite its successes, Ripple and XRP have also faced regulatory scrutiny, particularly from the U.S. Securities and Exchange Commission (SEC). The SEC's lawsuit against Ripple Labs has raised questions about the classification of XRP as a security, affecting its adoption and market perception. This ongoing legal battle underscores the complexities of navigating regulatory frameworks in the cryptocurrency space. As Ripple continues to evolve and adapt, understanding the historical context of XRP and its intended use case remains crucial for those looking to grasp its potential impact on the future of finance and cryptocurrency as a whole.

Understanding Digital Assets

Understanding digital assets is crucial for anyone delving into the world of cryptocurrencies, particularly XRP and its unique position within the financial ecosystem. Digital assets, in essence, are representations of value that exist in a digital format, secured by cryptography.

Unlike traditional assets, digital assets can offer enhanced transaction speed, lower costs, and increased accessibility. As cryptocurrencies continue to gain traction, their implications for various sectors, especially cross-border payments, become increasingly significant.

XRP, developed by Ripple Labs, is a prominent digital asset designed to facilitate fast and cost-effective cross-border transactions. Unlike Bitcoin, which is primarily a store of value, XRP serves as a bridge currency that enables financial institutions to transfer value in real-time. This functionality is particularly vital in an era where speed and efficiency are critical in financial transactions. By leveraging XRP, banks and payment providers can streamline their processes, reducing the need for pre-funded accounts and minimizing liquidity costs.

When comparing XRP to other cryptocurrencies, several distinguishing features emerge. While many cryptocurrencies operate on a decentralized model, XRP's consensus protocol allows for quicker transaction verification through a network of trusted validators. This design choice not only enhances speed but also results in lower energy consumption compared to proof-of-work cryptocurrencies like Bitcoin. Therefore, XRP is often viewed as a more environmentally friendly option, appealing to institutions that are increasingly conscious of their carbon footprints.

The technology behind XRP is rooted in its unique distributed ledger, known as the XRP Ledger. This ledger is designed for scalability and efficiency, supporting thousands of transactions per second. The XRP Ledger employs a consensus mechanism that does not require mining, which allows for faster transaction times. Understanding this technology is essential for grasping how XRP operates within the broader context of blockchain and cryptocurrency, especially as financial institutions explore innovative solutions for their payment systems.

XRP's integration within the realm of decentralized finance (DeFi) is also noteworthy. While DeFi has predominantly centered on Ethereum-based tokens, XRP's unique capabilities position it as a viable contender in this space. Through partnerships with various financial institutions, XRP is being utilized to enhance liquidity in DeFi applications, thereby bridging traditional finance with decentralized systems. This intersection of technologies offers exciting possibilities for the future of finance, making it imperative for anyone studying cryptocurrencies to comprehend the evolving role of digital assets like XRP in reshaping financial landscapes.

Chapter 2: XRP's Role in Cross-Border Payments

The Need for Efficient Cross-Border Transactions

In an increasingly globalized economy, the need for efficient cross-border transactions is more pressing than ever. Traditional banking systems often impose lengthy processing times and exorbitant fees for international transfers, creating obstacles for individuals and businesses alike. These inefficiencies can hinder economic growth, stifle innovation, and limit access to financial services for those in emerging markets. As the world shifts towards a more interconnected financial landscape, the demand for a streamlined and cost-effective solution has never been greater.

XRP, the digital asset associated with the Ripple network, emerges as a viable solution to these challenges. Utilizing blockchain technology, XRP enables near-instantaneous transactions across borders, significantly reducing the time it takes to settle payments. This speed is crucial for businesses engaged in international trade, as delays can result in lost opportunities and increased costs. By leveraging XRP, companies can facilitate seamless transactions, ensuring that payments reach their destination quickly and efficiently.

Moreover, the cost-effectiveness of using XRP for cross-border payments cannot be overlooked. Traditional remittance services often charge substantial fees, which can eat into the funds being transferred. In contrast, XRP transactions typically incur minimal fees, making it an attractive option for individuals and businesses looking to maximize their financial resources. This cost advantage not only benefits senders and recipients but also encourages more frequent cross-border transactions, ultimately driving economic activity and fostering global trade.

Additionally, XRP's ability to provide liquidity on demand plays a significant role in enhancing the efficiency of cross-border transactions. Unlike conventional payment systems that require pre-funding accounts in different currencies, XRP allows for real-time conversion between currencies, eliminating the need for intermediaries. This capability not only streamlines the payment process but also reduces the risk associated with currency fluctuations, providing users with greater certainty and predictability in their transactions.

As the world embraces digital transformation, the role of XRP in facilitating efficient cross-border transactions is becoming increasingly recognized. Financial institutions are exploring partnerships with Ripple to integrate XRP into their payment systems, enhancing their ability to serve customers in a fast-paced global market. The potential for XRP to revolutionize cross-border payments is immense, positioning it as a cornerstone in the evolving financial landscape and illustrating the broader implications of cryptocurrencies in driving economic progress.

How XRP Facilitates International Payments

XRP is designed to streamline and enhance the efficiency of international payments, addressing some of the longstanding challenges associated with cross-border transactions. Traditional methods of transferring money internationally often involve multiple intermediaries, high fees, and lengthy processing times. By utilizing XRP, financial institutions can facilitate these transactions in a more efficient manner, reducing costs and accelerating the speed at which funds are transferred across borders. This efficiency is crucial for businesses operating in a global market, where time and cost can significantly impact competitiveness.

One of the key advantages of XRP in international payments is its speed. Transactions using XRP are settled within seconds, regardless of the geographical distance between the sender and receiver. In contrast, traditional banking systems may take several days to process cross-border payments due to various factors, including time zone differences and the need for multiple banks to verify transactions. This swift settlement time allows businesses to manage their cash flow more effectively and respond to market demands promptly, enhancing their operational agility.

Additionally, XRP operates on a decentralized ledger technology known as the XRP Ledger, which ensures transparency and security in transactions. This ledger is maintained by a network of independent validators, which helps to prevent fraud and unauthorized transactions. The decentralized nature of the XRP Ledger means that it is not controlled by any single entity, reducing the risk associated with centralized financial systems. This trustworthiness is particularly appealing to financial institutions and businesses that require a reliable method for conducting international transactions.

XRP also addresses the issue of liquidity in cross-border payments. Traditional methods often require pre-funding accounts in different currencies, which can tie up capital and create inefficiencies. XRP provides a solution by allowing for on-demand liquidity, enabling institutions to convert their local currency to XRP and then to the destination currency, all in a matter of seconds. This not only reduces the need for pre-funded accounts but also minimizes foreign exchange risk, as transactions can be executed at favorable market rates.

In comparison to other cryptocurrencies, XRP stands out for its unique positioning in the cross-border payment space. While many cryptocurrencies focus on peer-to-peer transactions for individual users, XRP's primary aim is to serve financial institutions and facilitate large-scale international payments. This focus on partnerships with banks and payment providers has led to various use cases, with RippleNet, the network that utilizes XRP, gaining traction among global financial players. As the demand for efficient, reliable, and cost-effective international payment solutions continues to grow, XRP is poised to play a pivotal role in shaping the future of cross-border transactions.

Case Studies of XRP in Action

XRP has been at the forefront of innovative financial solutions, particularly in the realm of cross-border payments. One compelling case study is its partnership with MoneyGram, a global leader in remittances. In this collaboration, XRP is utilized to facilitate near-instantaneous transactions between different currencies. By leveraging Ripple's On-Demand Liquidity (ODL), MoneyGram can significantly reduce the time and cost associated with traditional money transfers, which often involve lengthy settlement periods and high fees. This case illustrates how XRP not only enhances the efficiency of transactions but also empowers businesses to operate on a global scale with greater agility.

Another notable example is the utilization of XRP by various financial institutions to streamline their payment processes. For instance, SBI Holdings in Japan has integrated XRP into its financial services, enabling faster and cost-effective international money transfers. Through this integration, SBI has been able to offer enhanced services to its clients, effectively demonstrating how traditional banking can benefit from adopting digital assets. This case study highlights the potential of XRP to bridge the gap between conventional finance and the emerging cryptocurrency ecosystem, showcasing its role in modernizing financial services.

XRP's functionality extends beyond individual partnerships to include its application in various industries. In the realm of supply chain management, companies have begun to explore the use of XRP for real-time tracking of payments and goods. By implementing XRP into their transaction systems, these companies can ensure transparency and traceability, reducing the risks associated with fraud and errors. This case exemplifies how XRP can serve multiple sectors, emphasizing its versatility and adaptability as a digital asset within different operational frameworks.

Moreover, the increasing adoption of XRP in the context of decentralized finance (DeFi) presents an intriguing case for its future potential. Platforms that utilize XRP allow users to engage in lending, borrowing, and trading without the need for traditional intermediaries. This not only democratizes access to financial services but also showcases XRP's ability to operate within a decentralized ecosystem. As more DeFi projects emerge and incorporate XRP, the asset's role in shaping the next generation of financial solutions becomes increasingly significant.

Finally, the comparative analysis of XRP against other cryptocurrencies offers insights into its unique strengths. Unlike Bitcoin or Ethereum, which face scalability issues and high transaction fees, XRP was designed for efficiency and speed. With its consensus algorithm facilitating rapid transaction confirmations, XRP stands out as a viable alternative for cross-border payments. This case study not only highlights XRP's advantages but also provides a broader understanding of its place within the cryptocurrency landscape, reinforcing its value proposition for both individuals and institutions seeking innovative financial solutions.

Chapter 3: XRP vs. Other Cryptocurrencies: A Comparative Analysis

Overview of Major Cryptocurrencies

The cryptocurrency landscape is diverse and dynamic, featuring a range of digital assets that serve various purposes. Among these, Bitcoin, Ethereum, and Ripple's XRP stand out as major players, each with unique attributes and uses. Bitcoin, introduced in 2009, is primarily recognized as a digital store of value and the first decentralized cryptocurrency. Its fixed supply and proof-of-work consensus mechanism underpin its value proposition as "digital gold." Ethereum, launched in 2015, expands on the concept of cryptocurrency by enabling smart contracts and decentralized applications (dApps) to be built on its blockchain, which has led to significant innovation in various sectors, including finance and gaming.

XRP, the digital asset associated with Ripple, is designed explicitly for facilitating cross-border payments. Unlike Bitcoin and Ethereum, which focus on decentralized transactions and programmable contracts, XRP aims to streamline and expedite international money transfers. Its consensus algorithm allows for quicker transaction validation and lower fees, making it an attractive alternative for financial institutions seeking to enhance their payment systems. This unique positioning makes XRP particularly relevant in discussions about improving the efficiency of global remittance networks and addressing the challenges of traditional banking systems.

In comparing XRP with other major cryptocurrencies, it is essential to consider their technological foundations and intended use cases. While Bitcoin's robust security and decentralized nature make it suitable for peer-to-peer transactions, Ethereum's programmable capabilities enable a wide range of decentralized applications. Conversely, XRP's centralized nature, managed by Ripple Labs, raises questions about its decentralization. However, this centralized approach allows for faster transaction processing, making XRP a favored choice among banks and payment providers looking to reduce costs and improve transaction speed in cross-border payments.

The technology behind XRP, particularly its distributed ledger technology, plays a crucial role in its functionality. RippleNet, the network that utilizes XRP, operates on a unique consensus protocol that allows participants to validate transactions without the need for mining. This efficiency not only reduces energy consumption but also enhances transaction speed, capable of settling in seconds. Understanding the mechanics of XRP's ledger is essential for grasping how it positions itself within the broader cryptocurrency ecosystem, especially as financial institutions look to leverage blockchain technology to modernize their operations.

Finally, XRP's role in the context of decentralized finance (DeFi) illustrates its versatility beyond traditional banking applications. While DeFi platforms predominantly utilize Ethereum and similar blockchains, Ripple's partnerships with various financial institutions highlight the potential for XRP to bridge traditional finance and DeFi solutions. XRP can facilitate liquidity and serve as a settlement asset, enabling financial institutions to engage with DeFi protocols. This intersection of XRP and DeFi demonstrates the evolving nature of cryptocurrencies and emphasizes the importance of understanding the broader implications of XRP within the financial landscape.

Comparing Transaction Speeds and Costs

In the realm of cryptocurrencies, transaction speed and cost are two critical factors that can significantly influence user experience and adoption. Ripple's digital asset, XRP, is often touted for its efficiency in these areas, especially when compared to other prominent cryptocurrencies like Bitcoin and Ethereum. To fully appreciate XRP's potential, it is essential to delve into how its transaction speeds and costs stack up against these alternatives, particularly in the context of cross-border payments, where efficiency is paramount.

XRP transactions are known for their remarkable speed, typically settling in about three to five seconds. This is a stark contrast to Bitcoin, which can take anywhere from ten minutes to several hours during peak congestion, and Ethereum, which usually takes around 15 seconds but can also experience delays due to network traffic. The rapid transaction times of XRP are primarily due to its unique consensus mechanism, which allows for quick validation of transactions without the need for extensive mining processes. This efficiency is particularly advantageous for financial institutions that require quick settlements to facilitate international transactions.

When it comes to transaction costs, XRP also stands out favorably. The average transaction fee for sending XRP is minimal, often costing fractions of a cent. In comparison, Bitcoin and Ethereum can incur much higher fees, especially during times of network congestion. For example, Bitcoin transaction fees can spike significantly, sometimes reaching upwards of $20, while Ethereum's fees can vary greatly depending on network demand and gas prices. The low cost of transactions in XRP makes it an appealing choice for both individuals and institutions looking to conduct frequent cross-border transactions without incurring substantial costs.

In addition to the benefits of speed and cost, XRP's design also plays a crucial role in enhancing its performance. The XRP Ledger employs a unique consensus algorithm that allows transactions to be verified by a network of validators rather than relying on traditional mining. This mechanism not only speeds up transaction times but also keeps costs low, as it reduces the computational power needed to process transactions. This efficient design positions XRP as a viable solution for businesses and financial institutions that require a reliable, fast, and cost-effective method for moving money across borders.

In conclusion, the comparative analysis of transaction speeds and costs reveals that XRP offers significant advantages over many other cryptocurrencies. Its ability to settle transactions quickly and affordably positions it as a leader in the cross-border payments space, attracting interest from financial institutions and users alike. As the cryptocurrency landscape continues to evolve, understanding these distinctions will be crucial for anyone looking to navigate the complexities of digital assets and their applications in real-world scenarios.

Security Features of XRP vs. Competitors

When exploring the security features of XRP, it is essential to compare them with those of other cryptocurrencies. Ripple's XRP is designed with a unique consensus algorithm that enhances its security and efficiency in processing transactions. Unlike Bitcoin and Ethereum, which rely on energy-intensive proof-of-work mechanisms, XRP employs a consensus protocol among trusted validators. This method not only speeds up transaction times to mere seconds but also reduces the risk of malicious attacks, making it a more secure option for cross-border payments.

XRP's architecture includes built-in mechanisms to prevent double-spending, a critical concern in digital currencies. The decentralized network of validators ensures that every transaction is verified by multiple parties before being added to the ledger. This system creates a robust layer of security that is less susceptible to manipulation compared to systems reliant on a single source of truth. In contrast, many other cryptocurrencies can be vulnerable to attacks if a majority of their mining power is compromised, leading to potential security breaches.

In addition to its consensus mechanism, XRP has a unique feature known as the "Escrow" function, which allows a predetermined amount of XRP to be locked away and released over time. This feature not only adds an extra layer of security to the asset but also ensures a controlled supply, mitigating the risk of sudden market fluctuations that can affect the stability of the currency. Many competitors lack such a feature, which can lead to more volatile price swings and increased risks for investors.

Another critical aspect of XRP's security is its response to regulatory challenges. Ripple has actively engaged with financial institutions and regulators worldwide to ensure compliance with existing laws. By fostering these relationships, XRP aims to create a secure environment for institutional adoption, which is often more challenging for other cryptocurrencies that operate in a more decentralized and less regulated manner. This proactive approach to regulation helps build trust among users and investors, further solidifying XRP's position as a secure choice for cross-border transactions.

When considering the security features of XRP in the context of decentralized finance (DeFi), it is important to highlight that while XRP is not typically included in the DeFi space, its underlying technology can support secure transactions within such frameworks. The transactional efficiency and security of XRP can potentially enhance DeFi applications, offering a safer alternative for users seeking to engage in lending, borrowing, and trading. As the DeFi ecosystem continues to evolve, the adoption of secure digital assets like XRP could play a significant role in shaping the future of secure financial transactions.

Use Cases and Adoption Rates

The adoption of XRP has been significantly influenced by its use cases, particularly in the realm of cross-border payments. Ripple, the company behind XRP, has developed a robust platform designed to facilitate fast and cost-effective transactions across different currencies. Financial institutions and payment providers have increasingly recognized the need for efficient solutions to handle international money transfers. XRP acts as a bridge currency, allowing for seamless exchanges without the need for multiple currency conversions, which can be time-consuming and expensive. This functionality has made XRP an attractive option for banks and payment services looking to enhance their operational efficiency.

In addition to its application in cross-border payments, XRP has garnered attention in the context of liquidity provisioning. Ripple's On-Demand Liquidity (ODL) service utilizes XRP to provide liquidity for transactions in real-time, eliminating the need for pre-funding accounts in destination currencies. This innovation is particularly beneficial for businesses operating in regions with limited access to traditional banking infrastructure. By reducing the capital requirements associated with maintaining foreign currency accounts, XRP enables companies to unlock their working capital, making it a practical choice for enterprises engaged in global trade.

The comparative analysis of XRP with other cryptocurrencies reveals its unique positioning within the digital asset ecosystem. While many cryptocurrencies serve primarily as speculative investments or store-of-value assets, XRP is designed specifically for utility in financial transactions. Its consensus algorithm, which differs from the proof-of-work and proof-of-stake mechanisms utilized by many other cryptocurrencies, allows for faster transaction speeds and lower energy consumption. This efficiency appeals to institutions that prioritize scalability and sustainability, making XRP a preferred choice in sectors that require high transaction throughput.

Partnerships between Ripple and financial institutions further underscore the real-world use of XRP. Major banks and payment providers, including Santander and American Express, have explored or implemented Ripple's technology to streamline their operations. These collaborations illustrate the growing trust in XRP's potential to revolutionize traditional banking practices. As these institutions adopt XRP and its underlying technology, they not only enhance their own service offerings but also contribute to the overall adoption and legitimacy of XRP in the financial ecosystem.

Lastly, the emergence of decentralized finance (DeFi) presents both challenges and opportunities for XRP. While DeFi primarily focuses on creating decentralized financial services using blockchain technology, XRP is exploring ways to integrate into this evolving landscape. The potential for interoperability between XRP and various DeFi platforms could enable users to leverage XRP's liquidity and speed in decentralized applications. As the DeFi space continues to grow, XRP's unique characteristics and established partnerships may position it as a valuable asset in this new financial paradigm, further driving its adoption and use cases across diverse sectors.

Chapter 4: The Technology Behind XRP: Understanding the Ledger

Introduction to the XRP Ledger

The XRP Ledger, often referred to as the XRPL, is a decentralized blockchain technology that underpins the digital asset XRP. Launched in 2012 by Ripple Labs, the XRPL is designed to facilitate fast and cost-effective cross-border transactions. Unlike some other blockchain networks that utilize proof-of-work or proof-of-stake consensus mechanisms, the XRP Ledger employs a unique consensus protocol, enabling it to process transactions in mere seconds. This rapid transaction speed, combined with low fees, positions the XRPL as a viable solution for financial institutions looking to optimize global payment systems.

At its core, the XRP Ledger is an open-source platform, meaning that it is accessible to anyone who wishes to participate in its network or develop applications on top of it. This transparency fosters trust and innovation within the ecosystem. The ledger operates through a network of independent validators that reach consensus on the state of the ledger, ensuring the integrity of transactions without the need for a central authority. The decentralized nature of the XRPL not only enhances security but also reduces the risks associated with central points of failure, making it a robust alternative in the ever-evolving landscape of digital finance.

One of the most significant advantages of the XRP Ledger is its ability to facilitate cross-border payments. Traditional methods of transferring funds internationally are often slow and costly due to various intermediaries and currency conversions. The XRPL streamlines this process by enabling direct transfers between parties, significantly reducing transaction times and costs. This capability is particularly appealing to financial institutions that seek to improve their services in a competitive market. By utilizing the XRPL, banks and payment providers can enhance their transaction efficiency, ultimately benefiting their customers.

The technology behind the XRP Ledger is a critical aspect that sets it apart from other cryptocurrencies. While many digital currencies operate on a purely transactional basis, the XRPL incorporates features like smart contracts and decentralized applications (dApps), which broaden its functionality. These capabilities allow developers to create innovative solutions, paving the way for new financial products and services. Understanding the underlying technology of the XRPL is essential for anyone looking to grasp the full potential of XRP and its applications within the financial sector.

As the cryptocurrency landscape evolves, the role of XRP within decentralized finance (DeFi) is becoming increasingly prominent. By integrating with various DeFi platforms and projects, the XRP Ledger is positioning itself as a crucial player in the future of finance. Its compatibility with diverse financial applications allows for enhanced liquidity, lending, and trading possibilities. Additionally, partnerships with established financial institutions further validate the XRPL's potential, showcasing its ability to bridge the gap between traditional finance and the burgeoning world of cryptocurrencies. This intersection marks a transformative shift in how value is transferred globally, making the study of the XRP Ledger essential for anyone interested in the future of digital assets.

Consensus Mechanism Explained

Consensus mechanisms are foundational to the operation of cryptocurrencies, including XRP. They are methodologies used to achieve agreement among distributed systems, ensuring that all participants in a network can trust the integrity of the data being processed. In the context of XRP, the consensus mechanism is critical for validating transactions and maintaining the integrity of the XRP Ledger. Unlike Bitcoin, which relies on proof of work, XRP employs a unique consensus protocol that allows for quicker transaction processing and lower energy consumption.

The XRP Ledger utilizes a consensus algorithm known as the Ripple Protocol Consensus Algorithm (RPCA). This mechanism operates through a network of validators, which are nodes that agree on the order and validity of transactions. Validators do not compete to solve complex mathematical problems, as seen in traditional proof-of-work systems. Instead, they work collaboratively to verify transactions and reach consensus on the state of the ledger. This approach not only enhances efficiency but also reduces the time required for transaction confirmations, making XRP particularly suitable for cross-border payments.

Each validator operates independently and maintains its own copy of the ledger. Periodically, the validators convene to reach an agreement on the current state of the ledger. They do this by examining proposed transactions and deciding which should be included in the next ledger version. A unique aspect of the RPCA is the concept of "trusted validators." Users can choose a set of trusted validators based on their preferences, allowing for a level of customization in the consensus process. This flexibility contributes to the overall resilience of the network while ensuring that transactions are processed swiftly and reliably.

The efficiency of Ripple's consensus mechanism contributes significantly to XRP's role in cross-border payments. Traditional systems often face delays and high transaction fees due to the reliance on intermediary banks and lengthy processing times. In contrast, XRP transactions can be settled in mere seconds, with minimal costs. This capability positions XRP as a viable alternative for financial institutions looking to streamline their cross-border payment processes, ultimately enhancing global financial transactions.

In the broader cryptocurrency landscape, the consensus mechanism used by XRP differentiates it from other cryptocurrencies. While many cryptocurrencies grapple with scalability issues and energy consumption, XRP's RPCA presents a compelling solution. The combination of speed, cost-effectiveness, and energy efficiency makes XRP an attractive option for both individuals and institutions. As the cryptocurrency market continues to evolve, understanding the nuances of consensus mechanisms like those used in XRP will be vital for anyone seeking to navigate the complexities of digital assets and their applications in decentralized finance.

Benefits of the XRP Ledger Technology

The XRP Ledger technology offers a range of benefits that make it a standout choice in the ever-evolving landscape of cryptocurrencies. One of the primary advantages is its speed and efficiency in processing transactions. The XRP Ledger can settle transactions in just a few seconds, which is significantly faster than many blockchain networks. This rapid transaction time is particularly advantageous for cross-border payments, where traditional banking systems can take days to finalize transactions. By streamlining the payment process, the XRP Ledger enhances liquidity and reduces the costs associated with currency exchange.

Another significant benefit of the XRP Ledger is its low transaction costs. The fees associated with transactions on the XRP Ledger are minimal, often costing a fraction of a cent. This affordability opens the door for microtransactions, enabling new use cases that would be impractical on other platforms with higher fees. For businesses and individuals alike, the reduced cost of conducting transactions makes the XRP Ledger an attractive option for both everyday transactions and large-scale financial operations.

The technology behind the XRP Ledger is also noteworthy for its scalability. As the number of users and transactions grows, the XRP Ledger can handle increased demand without sacrificing speed or efficiency. This scalability is essential for financial institutions and businesses operating in dynamic environments where transaction volumes can fluctuate dramatically. It positions the XRP Ledger as a viable solution for both current and future demands in the digital asset space, making it appealing to a wide range of users.

Furthermore, the XRP Ledger is built with a focus on security and decentralization. The consensus mechanism employed by the XRP Ledger ensures that transactions are validated by a network of independent validators, minimizing the risk of fraud or double-spending. This robust security framework not only protects users but also enhances trust in the network, making it a suitable choice for financial institutions that prioritize regulatory compliance and security in their operations.

Lastly, the XRP Ledger supports a diverse ecosystem of applications and use cases beyond just payments. Its ability to facilitate smart contracts and tokenization allows developers to build innovative solutions that leverage its underlying technology. This versatility has led to partnerships with various financial institutions and businesses exploring ways to integrate the XRP Ledger into their operations. As decentralized finance (DeFi) continues to grow, the XRP Ledger's capabilities position it as a key player, offering unique opportunities for innovation within the financial landscape.

Chapter 5: XRP and Financial Institutions: Partnerships and Use Cases

Overview of Ripple's Partnerships

Ripple has established a robust network of partnerships that play a crucial role in the adoption and integration of its digital asset, XRP, within the global financial ecosystem. These collaborations span various sectors, including banks, payment providers, and fintech companies, all aimed at enhancing cross-border payment solutions. By working with a diverse array of institutions, Ripple aims to streamline and modernize the way money moves across borders, addressing the inefficiencies that have long plagued traditional banking systems.

One of the most significant aspects of Ripple's partnerships is its focus on traditional financial institutions. Ripple has collaborated with major banks and payment service providers, which lends credibility to its technology and fosters trust in XRP as a viable medium for cross-border transactions. Institutions like Santander, American Express, and SBI Holdings have all embraced Ripple's technology, leveraging its capabilities to facilitate faster and cheaper international payments. These partnerships not only showcase the potential of XRP but also highlight the growing acceptance of blockchain technology within established financial frameworks.

Additionally, Ripple's partnerships extend to a variety of payment networks and remittance services, enhancing the accessibility of XRP in everyday transactions. Collaborations with companies like MoneyGram have enabled Ripple to integrate its technology into existing payment infrastructures, allowing for seamless transactions between users. This synergy not only improves the efficiency of cross-border payments but also demonstrates how XRP can be utilized in real-world applications, making it an attractive option for remittance services looking to reduce costs and increase transaction speeds.

The strategic alliances formed by Ripple also include partnerships with technology firms and blockchain-based projects. By aligning with innovators in the tech space, Ripple enhances its technological capabilities and expands its reach within the cryptocurrency ecosystem. These collaborations often focus on developing new use cases for XRP, such as facilitating decentralized finance (DeFi) applications or integrating with other blockchain networks. Such partnerships are vital as they help Ripple stay competitive in a rapidly evolving market, ensuring that XRP remains relevant and adaptable to changing technological landscapes.

In summary, the overview of Ripple's partnerships highlights the organization's commitment to revolutionizing cross-border payments through collaboration with various stakeholders. By fostering relationships with banks, payment providers, and technology firms, Ripple is not only promoting the use of XRP but also driving the broader acceptance of blockchain technology in financial transactions. These partnerships are instrumental in positioning XRP as a leading digital asset in the evolving landscape of cryptocurrencies, paving the way for a future where cross-border payments are more efficient, transparent, and accessible.

Use Cases in Banking and Financial Services

In the banking and financial services sectors, XRP has begun to carve a significant niche, primarily due to its unique attributes that facilitate faster and more cost-effective transactions compared to traditional systems. One of the most prominent use cases is in cross-border payments, where XRP serves as a bridge currency. This capability allows financial institutions to settle transactions instantly, bypassing the lengthy processes typically associated with international transfers. By utilizing XRP, banks can reduce the reliance on pre-funded accounts in destination currencies, thereby optimizing liquidity management and minimizing operational costs.

Another key use case for XRP in financial services is in remittances. Traditional remittance methods often involve high fees and delays, which can be particularly burdensome for individuals sending money across borders. With XRP, remittance companies can offer their customers a more efficient alternative, ensuring that funds are transferred quickly and inexpensively. This improvement not only enhances customer experience but also opens new avenues for businesses to operate more effectively in global markets, ultimately fostering a more inclusive financial ecosystem.

XRP also plays a crucial role in enhancing the efficiency of payment processing systems. Financial institutions can leverage XRP to streamline their operations, significantly reducing settlement times from days to a matter of seconds. This instantaneous nature of transactions enables banks to provide better services to their customers, such as real-time payments and improved cash flow management. Moreover, the ability to conduct transactions 24/7 without the constraints of traditional banking hours positions XRP as a transformative asset in the financial landscape.

Beyond payment processing, XRP is increasingly being integrated into regulatory compliance frameworks within financial institutions. The transparency and traceability provided by the XRP Ledger make it an ideal candidate for Know Your Customer (KYC) and Anti-Money Laundering (AML) practices. By using XRP, banks can enhance their compliance measures while simultaneously reducing the costs associated with manual compliance processes. This level of efficiency not only mitigates risks but also fosters trust between financial institutions and their customers.

Finally, the partnerships that Ripple, the company behind XRP, has forged with various financial institutions underscore the practical applications of XRP in banking and finance. Collaborations with banks and payment providers globally have demonstrated the versatility and reliability of XRP in real-world scenarios. As the landscape of financial services continues to evolve, XRP's role is likely to expand further, solidifying its position as a foundational asset in the realm of digital currencies and driving innovation across the industry.

The Impact of XRP on Global Finance

The impact of XRP on global finance is significant, particularly in the realm of cross-border payments. As a digital asset designed specifically for facilitating international transactions, XRP provides a solution to the traditional inefficiencies associated with transferring money across borders. Traditional banking systems often rely on a series of intermediaries to process these transactions, which can result in long wait times and high fees. By using XRP, financial institutions can bypass many of these obstacles, allowing for near-instantaneous transfers and reduced costs. This efficiency is crucial for businesses that operate globally, as it enables them to manage cash flow more effectively and enhance their competitiveness in the market.

XRP's role in cross-border payments is underscored by its partnership with various financial institutions worldwide. Ripple, the company behind XRP, has established numerous collaborations with banks and payment service providers to integrate its technology into their systems. These partnerships have demonstrated the practical applications of XRP in real-world financial transactions, showcasing its ability to streamline processes and improve the overall experience for both consumers and businesses. As more institutions recognize the advantages of utilizing XRP, its adoption is likely to increase, further solidifying its position in the global financial landscape.

When comparing XRP to other cryptocurrencies, it is essential to consider its unique attributes and use cases. Unlike Bitcoin and Ethereum, which are primarily viewed as store-of-value or smart contract platforms, XRP was specifically developed to address the needs of the financial sector. Its consensus algorithm allows for faster transaction validation and lower energy consumption compared to proof-of-work systems. This makes XRP particularly appealing to financial institutions seeking a sustainable and efficient digital asset for their operations. As the cryptocurrency market evolves, XRP's distinct focus on financial services may position it favorably against its more generalized counterparts.

Understanding the technology behind XRP is crucial for grasping its potential impact on global finance. The XRP Ledger is an open-source blockchain that supports high transaction throughput and low latency. This technology enables institutions to conduct a large number of transactions simultaneously without compromising security. Additionally, the decentralized nature of the ledger ensures transparency and reduces the risk of fraud, which is paramount in financial transactions. As more financial entities explore blockchain technology, the advantages of the XRP Ledger may drive further adoption and innovation within the sector.

In the context of decentralized finance (DeFi), XRP's influence is also worth noting. While DeFi has gained momentum primarily through platforms built on Ethereum, XRP's integration into this space presents unique opportunities. By facilitating cross-border transactions and liquidity provision, XRP can enhance DeFi applications, bridging traditional finance with innovative financial solutions. The collaboration between XRP and DeFi platforms could lead to new financial products and services that leverage the strengths of both worlds, ultimately contributing to a more inclusive and efficient financial ecosystem. As users continue to seek alternatives to conventional banking, XRP's role in this evolving landscape is poised to be transformative.

Chapter 6: XRP in the Context of Decentralized Finance (DeFi)

Understanding DeFi and its Significance

Decentralized Finance, commonly referred to as DeFi, represents a transformative approach to financial services, leveraging blockchain technology to create an open and permissionless financial system. Unlike traditional finance, which relies on intermediaries like banks and brokers, DeFi utilizes smart contracts on blockchain networks to facilitate transactions and services directly between users. This paradigm shift has the potential to democratize access to financial products, allowing individuals to engage in lending, borrowing, trading, and earning interest without the constraints of centralized authorities.

One of the primary significance of DeFi lies in its ability to provide financial services to the unbanked and underbanked populations around the world. With over a billion people lacking access to traditional banking systems, DeFi platforms offer an alternative by enabling users to interact with financial instruments directly through their smartphones or computers. By removing the barriers imposed by banks, DeFi empowers individuals to manage their finances autonomously, fostering greater financial inclusion and participation in the global economy.

In the context of Ripple and its digital asset XRP, DeFi holds particular relevance. Ripple has been at the forefront of developing solutions for cross-border payments, and as DeFi continues to evolve, the interplay between XRP and DeFi applications becomes increasingly significant. XRP can be utilized within DeFi protocols to facilitate instant, low-cost transactions, enhancing liquidity and interoperability across diverse platforms. This capability positions XRP as a valuable asset within the DeFi ecosystem, furthering its utility beyond mere speculative investment.

Moreover, DeFi introduces innovative financial products that challenge traditional models, such as yield farming, liquidity pools, and decentralized exchanges. These mechanisms allow users to earn returns on their assets by providing liquidity to various DeFi protocols. As XRP gains traction within these frameworks, it may attract users seeking to capitalize on DeFi opportunities, thus expanding its use cases and fostering a more vibrant ecosystem centered around Ripple's technology.

In summary, understanding DeFi and its significance is essential for anyone exploring the landscape of cryptocurrencies, particularly in relation to XRP. As DeFi continues to reshape the financial industry, its integration with digital assets like XRP not only enhances the asset's functionality but also highlights the broader potential of blockchain technology in creating a more inclusive and efficient financial system. This dynamic interplay will be pivotal in driving innovation and adoption, ultimately influencing the future of both Ripple and the global financial ecosystem.

XRP's Place in the DeFi Ecosystem

XRP occupies a unique and significant position within the decentralized finance (DeFi) ecosystem, primarily due to its speed, scalability, and low transaction costs. While DeFi is predominantly associated with Ethereum-based tokens and platforms, XRP's underlying technology and use cases extend its relevance beyond traditional boundaries. The ability of XRP to facilitate quick and cost-effective transactions makes it an attractive option for users seeking to engage in DeFi activities, such as lending, borrowing, and trading, without the high fees often associated with other cryptocurrencies.

One of the most notable contributions of XRP to the DeFi landscape is its interoperability with various financial systems. Unlike many DeFi projects that are confined to specific blockchain networks, XRP can be integrated with multiple platforms, providing users with seamless access to liquidity pools and decentralized exchanges. This interoperability enhances the overall efficiency of DeFi applications, allowing users to leverage XRP for cross-chain transactions, which can significantly improve the user experience and reduce the time required to execute trades and transfers.

The use of XRP in DeFi also brings forth the concept of liquidity provisioning. XRP's inherent characteristics, such as its rapid settlement times and low volatility, make it an ideal asset for liquidity providers in decentralized exchanges. By utilizing XRP, liquidity providers can attract more users and enhance trading volumes, thereby creating a more robust marketplace. This increased liquidity not only benefits individual users but also contributes to the overall health and stability of the DeFi ecosystem, encouraging further innovation and development.

Moreover, XRP's role in DeFi extends to lending and borrowing protocols. Many platforms are beginning to adopt XRP as collateral, allowing users to secure loans with their holdings while still participating in other DeFi opportunities. This functionality empowers users to optimize their financial strategies, enabling them to generate passive income through interest while retaining access to their XRP assets. Such integrations highlight the versatility of XRP and its potential to support a diverse range of financial products within the DeFi space.

Lastly, as regulatory frameworks around cryptocurrencies continue to evolve, XRP's established presence in the financial sector may provide an added layer of legitimacy to DeFi projects that incorporate it. Partnerships with financial institutions and compliance with regulatory standards can instill a sense of trust among users wary of the risks associated with DeFi. As the landscape matures, XRP's integration into DeFi could play a crucial role in bridging the gap between traditional finance and the decentralized world, ultimately driving broader adoption and innovation within both realms.

Future Prospects for XRP in DeFi

As decentralized finance (DeFi) continues to gain traction within the cryptocurrency ecosystem, the future prospects for XRP in this rapidly evolving landscape are becoming increasingly significant. XRP, known for its efficiency and speed in cross-border payments, has the potential to bridge the gap between traditional financial systems and DeFi platforms. With its unique technological framework, XRP can facilitate seamless transactions and liquidity, making it an attractive option for projects aiming to innovate within the DeFi space.

The integration of XRP into DeFi could address several pain points currently faced by traditional finance. For instance, the slow transaction speeds and high fees associated with conventional banking can be mitigated by utilizing XRP's capabilities. This could enhance user experience and allow for more efficient decentralized applications (dApps), further promoting the adoption of DeFi solutions. Additionally, XRP's liquidity can be a valuable asset for liquidity pools and decentralized exchanges, creating a more robust ecosystem that encourages participation from both individual users and institutional players.

XRP's unique consensus mechanism, which relies on a network of validators rather than traditional mining, positions it as an environmentally friendly option in the DeFi arena. With growing concerns over the sustainability of proof-of-work and other energy-intensive blockchain technologies, XRP's low energy consumption could appeal to eco-conscious developers and investors. This aspect may also contribute to the broader acceptance of XRP among DeFi enthusiasts who are increasingly prioritizing sustainability in their investment choices.

Partnerships with financial institutions and established projects in the DeFi space could further enhance XRP's role in this domain. Ripple has already formed strategic alliances with various banks and payment providers, and leveraging these relationships could facilitate the development of hybrid solutions that combine traditional finance with DeFi. By collaborating with DeFi platforms, Ripple could help foster innovation while simultaneously addressing regulatory concerns, thus driving greater acceptance of XRP in the decentralized finance ecosystem.

Looking ahead, the regulatory environment will play a crucial role in shaping the future of XRP within DeFi. As governments worldwide develop frameworks to govern cryptocurrencies, clarity around XRP's legal status will be essential for its integration into DeFi projects. A favorable regulatory outlook could not only bolster confidence among developers and investors but also drive the creation of compliant DeFi solutions that utilize XRP for transactions and smart contracts. As the DeFi landscape matures, XRP's adaptability and established infrastructure may position it as a pivotal player in the ongoing transformation of finance.

Chapter 7: Investing in XRP

How to Buy and Store XRP

When considering the acquisition of XRP, it is essential to start with a reputable cryptocurrency exchange. Exchanges like Coinbase, Binance, and Kraken offer a user-friendly platform for buying XRP. Each exchange has its own set of features, fees, and security measures, so it is important to research and select one that aligns with your preferences. After creating an account, you will typically need to complete a verification process, which may involve providing identification and proof of residence. Once your account is set up, you can fund it using various payment methods such as bank transfers, credit cards, or even other cryptocurrencies.

After funding your account, you can navigate to the XRP trading section of the exchange. Here, you can place a market order, which allows you to buy XRP at the current market price, or a limit order, where you can specify the price at which you are willing to buy. It's advisable to start with a smaller amount until you become familiar with the trading process and the volatility often associated with cryptocurrency markets. Once your purchase is completed, the XRP will be credited to your exchange wallet, but it is generally recommended to transfer your assets to a private wallet for enhanced security.

Storing XRP securely is crucial to safeguarding your investment. There are several options available, including hardware wallets, software wallets, and exchanges' wallets. Hardware wallets, such as Ledger or Trezor, are considered one of the safest options as they store your private keys offline, thus minimizing the risk of hacking. Software wallets, which can be desktop or mobile applications, offer more convenience but may expose your assets to online threats. For those who choose to keep their XRP on an exchange, it is important to select exchanges with strong security measures, including two-factor authentication and insurance policies.

Setting up a private wallet involves generating a wallet address, which is essential for receiving XRP. Various wallet options support XRP, and selecting one that suits your needs is critical. Ensure that you back up your wallet's recovery phrase securely, as losing this could result in the total loss of your funds. Additionally, keeping your wallet software up to date helps protect against vulnerabilities. Regularly reviewing your security practices, such as enabling two-factor authentication and monitoring your accounts for unusual activity, is advisable.

In summary, buying and storing XRP involves choosing a reputable exchange, executing your purchase, and securely storing your assets. As you navigate the world of cryptocurrencies, understanding the importance of security and the different storage options can help you manage your XRP effectively. Being informed about these processes will not only enhance your confidence in handling XRP but also prepare you for its potential role in cross-border payments and its comparative advantages over other cryptocurrencies. Always stay updated on market trends and security practices to ensure a successful experience in the cryptocurrency landscape.

Risks and Considerations

When exploring XRP and its potential as a digital asset, it is essential to consider the various risks and factors that may impact its adoption and value. One of the primary risks involves regulatory scrutiny. Governments and financial regulators worldwide are still trying to understand how cryptocurrencies fit into existing financial systems. XRP, being linked to Ripple Labs, has faced scrutiny regarding its classification as a security or a currency, which can influence its market perception and legality in different jurisdictions. Investors and users should stay informed about regulatory developments, as these can dramatically affect the operational landscape for XRP.

Market volatility presents another significant risk for those interested in XRP. The cryptocurrency market is known for its price fluctuations, which can be driven by a myriad of factors, including market sentiment, technological advancements, and broader economic trends. XRP is no exception to this volatility. The rapid rise or fall in price can lead to substantial gains or losses for investors. Understanding the historical price trends and market dynamics is crucial for anyone considering investing in or utilizing XRP for transactions, particularly in the context of cross-border payments where stability is often a priority.

Technological risks also warrant attention, especially regarding the underlying blockchain technology that supports XRP. While the XRP Ledger is designed to handle transactions quickly and efficiently, it is not immune to potential technical issues, such as network outages, bugs, or vulnerabilities. Additionally, as the technology landscape evolves, new innovations or competing solutions could emerge, potentially impacting XRP's market position. Users must keep abreast of technological developments and be prepared for the implications they may have on the functionality and security of XRP.

Another consideration is the competitive landscape of cryptocurrencies. XRP does not exist in a vacuum; it is part of a larger ecosystem that includes Bitcoin, Ethereum, and various other altcoins. Each of these cryptocurrencies has unique features and uses, which can create challenges for XRP in terms of market adoption and user preference. An informed analysis of how XRP compares with other digital assets, especially in the context of cross-border payments and decentralized finance, is vital for understanding its potential role and limitations in the broader market.

Finally, the involvement of financial institutions presents both opportunities and risks for XRP. While Ripple has secured partnerships with several banks and payment providers, the success of these collaborations is not guaranteed. The willingness of traditional financial institutions to adopt XRP as a payment solution may vary, influenced by factors such as institutional risk appetite, regulatory compliance, and competitive pressures. As the landscape of financial services evolves, the interplay between XRP and established financial entities will be a critical aspect for users to consider when evaluating its long-term viability and relevance in the world of digital assets.

Long-Term vs. Short-Term Investment Strategies

Long-term and short-term investment strategies are essential concepts for anyone engaging with cryptocurrencies, including Ripple's XRP. Understanding the differences between these approaches can significantly impact an investor's experience and outcomes. Long-term investment strategies typically involve holding an asset for an extended period, often years, with the expectation that its value will increase over time. This approach suits investors who believe in the fundamental value of XRP and its potential role in revolutionizing cross-border payments and financial transactions. By analyzing XRP's technology and its partnerships with financial institutions, investors can identify its long-term viability.

In contrast, short-term investment strategies focus on taking advantage of price fluctuations over shorter periods, such as days or weeks. This approach requires a keen understanding of market trends, news cycles, and technical analysis. For XRP investors employing this strategy, the volatile nature of the cryptocurrency market can present opportunities for profit through quick trades. However, short-term trading can also introduce significant risks, especially in a market as unpredictable as cryptocurrency. Therefore, it is crucial for investors to stay informed about developments surrounding XRP and its competitive landscape to make informed decisions.

When considering these strategies, it is important to evaluate one's risk tolerance and investment goals. Long-term investors in XRP may prioritize stability and gradual growth, aligning their decisions with the broader trends in digital finance and the increasing adoption of blockchain technology. Such investors might focus on XRP's role in facilitating faster and cheaper cross-border payments and its partnerships with banks and financial institutions. Conversely, short-term investors may prioritize maximizing returns by capitalizing on market sentiments, necessitating a more active monitoring of XRP's price movements.

The decision between long-term and short-term strategies may also be influenced by the overall market conditions. In bullish markets, where prices are generally rising, long-term holders might see substantial gains without the need for constant trading. However, in bearish or highly volatile markets, short-term strategies may offer a way to mitigate losses or capitalize on rapid price changes. Investors should consider these dynamics when deciding how to approach their investments in XRP and other cryptocurrencies.

Ultimately, the choice between long-term and short-term investment strategies in the context of XRP should be based on individual circumstances and preferences. Some investors may find a hybrid approach beneficial, combining aspects of both strategies to achieve their financial objectives. As the cryptocurrency landscape continues to evolve, understanding these investment strategies can empower individuals to navigate the complexities of XRP and its potential within the broader financial ecosystem.

Chapter 8: The Future of XRP and Ripple

Market Trends and Predictions

Market trends in the cryptocurrency landscape have shown remarkable evolution over the past few years, with XRP positioning itself as a significant player, particularly in the realm of cross-border payments. Ripple's digital asset has garnered attention not only for its speed and efficiency but also for its unique consensus mechanism, which sets it apart from traditional cryptocurrencies like Bitcoin and Ethereum. As financial institutions increasingly recognize the potential of blockchain technology to streamline transactions, XRP's role in facilitating these processes is expected to expand. This trend is likely to continue, driven by the growing demand for faster and more cost-effective cross-border payment solutions.

The competitive landscape for cryptocurrencies is also evolving, with a notable shift towards regulatory clarity and institutional adoption. XRP has maintained a competitive edge against other digital assets due to its strategic partnerships with banks and financial service providers. These collaborations have allowed XRP to integrate seamlessly into existing financial systems, enhancing its viability as a bridge currency. As more institutions explore the use of cryptocurrencies for remittances and international trade, XRP is well-positioned to capture a significant share of this expanding market, particularly as regulatory frameworks become more defined.

Technological advancements play a crucial role in shaping market trends. The XRP Ledger, known for its scalability and energy efficiency, continues to attract interest from developers and businesses alike. The ledger's ability to settle transactions in mere seconds appeals to those seeking to implement real-time payment solutions. As decentralized finance (DeFi) gains traction, the interoperability of XRP with various blockchain networks could lead to innovative use cases that enhance liquidity and accessibility across the financial ecosystem. This potential for integration with DeFi protocols is likely to influence market sentiment positively, drawing more users to XRP.

Investor sentiment in the cryptocurrency market is notoriously volatile, influenced by both macroeconomic factors and technological developments. As the landscape continues to mature, the need for robust analysis and prediction models becomes paramount. Analysts are increasingly focusing on the long-term potential of digital assets like XRP, particularly in light of its unique attributes and established partnerships. Predictions suggest that as global financial systems increasingly embrace digital currencies, XRP could see significant appreciation, assuming it effectively navigates regulatory challenges and maintains its competitive advantages.

Looking forward, the intersection of XRP with evolving market trends presents a complex but promising picture. With the rise of digital currencies being embraced by central banks and financial institutions, XRP's role may expand beyond mere cross-border payments to encompass a broader range of financial services. This could include enhanced liquidity provision, integration into new financial products, and participation in emerging markets. As the cryptocurrency landscape continues to evolve, XRP's adaptability and strategic positioning will be critical factors in determining its future trajectory and relevance in the digital asset economy.

Regulatory Challenges Ahead

Regulatory challenges are a significant consideration for any cryptocurrency, and XRP is no exception. As a digital asset designed primarily for cross-border payments, XRP operates in a landscape that is heavily influenced by the legal and regulatory frameworks established by various governments and financial authorities. The evolving nature of these regulations creates uncertainty not only for Ripple, the company behind XRP, but also for its users and potential investors. Understanding these regulatory challenges is crucial for anyone looking to navigate the world of XRP and its broader implications in the cryptocurrency ecosystem.

One of the primary regulatory hurdles facing XRP is the classification of the asset itself. Regulators around the world have differing opinions on whether XRP should be considered a security, a commodity, or something entirely different. In the United States, the Securities and Exchange Commission (SEC) has notably taken a firm stance, arguing that XRP is a security and falls under its jurisdiction. This classification has significant implications for Ripple and its ability to operate freely in the market, as well as for XRP holders who may be concerned about the legal status of their assets.

Internationally, the regulatory landscape is equally complex. Different jurisdictions have implemented various frameworks for cryptocurrencies, ranging from outright bans to more permissive approaches. For XRP to achieve its full potential in facilitating cross-border payments, it must navigate these differing regulations. The challenge lies in ensuring compliance while promoting innovation, as overly stringent regulations could stifle the growth of the cryptocurrency ecosystem and inhibit the development of new financial technologies that utilize XRP.

Moreover, regulatory challenges extend beyond classification and compliance. There is also the issue of anti-money laundering (AML) and know your customer (KYC) regulations, which are increasingly being applied to cryptocurrencies. Financial institutions partnering with Ripple must ensure that their use of XRP complies with these regulations to avoid legal repercussions. This adds another layer of complexity for XRP's adoption in traditional finance, as companies must balance regulatory requirements with the benefits of using a digital asset for payments.

Lastly, the ongoing discussions around stablecoins and central bank digital currencies (CBDCs) further complicate the regulatory environment for XRP. As governments explore the creation of their own digital currencies, the competitive landscape for cross-border payments may shift dramatically. This could lead to new regulations that impact how XRP is perceived and utilized. Understanding these dynamics is essential for those interested in XRP, as the regulatory challenges ahead will shape not only the future of this digital asset but also its role in the broader financial ecosystem.

The Vision for Ripple and XRP

The vision for Ripple and its digital asset XRP is deeply rooted in the ambition to transform the global financial landscape. Ripple was established with the intent to create a seamless, efficient, and cost-effective solution for cross-border payments. Unlike traditional banking systems, which often involve multiple intermediaries and significant delays, Ripple aims to facilitate instant transactions that can be settled in real time. This vision positions XRP as a crucial component of Ripple's broader mission, providing liquidity and enabling faster settlement times for financial institutions around the world.

At the core of this vision is the recognition of the challenges faced by the current cross-border payment systems. Traditional methods can be sluggish and expensive, leading to frustrations for businesses and consumers alike. Ripple's technology seeks to address these pain points by utilizing blockchain to streamline transactions. By integrating XRP into its network, Ripple enhances the efficiency of cross-border payments, allowing institutions to send and receive money across borders with minimal friction. This approach not only reduces transaction costs but also increases transparency, making it an attractive option for financial institutions looking to modernize their payment systems.

When comparing XRP to other cryptocurrencies, it is essential to understand its unique attributes and intended use case. While many cryptocurrencies are designed primarily as speculative assets, XRP's primary function is to serve as a bridge currency in international transactions. This distinct role sets XRP apart, as it is not just another digital asset but a tool that facilitates the movement of value across different fiat currencies. Ripple's strategic partnerships with banks and payment providers further reinforce this vision, as they work collaboratively to implement XRP in practical use cases, enhancing its viability in the financial sector.

The technology behind XRP, particularly the XRP Ledger, is also a fundamental aspect of Ripple's vision. The XRP Ledger operates with a consensus protocol that enables secure and rapid transaction processing without relying on traditional mining mechanisms. This technology ensures that transactions are validated efficiently, allowing for a high throughput of transactions per second. By utilizing this innovative ledger technology, Ripple not only enhances the speed and efficiency of payments but also positions XRP as a sustainable and eco-friendly alternative to other cryptocurrencies that require substantial energy consumption for mining.

As the landscape of decentralized finance (DeFi) continues to evolve, XRP's role within this context is gaining attention. Ripple's vision extends beyond just cross-border payments; it encompasses a broader ambition to integrate with DeFi platforms, thereby expanding the utility of XRP. By enabling interoperability between various financial services, Ripple aims to create an inclusive ecosystem where XRP can facilitate lending, borrowing, and trading across decentralized networks. This vision not only enhances the functionality of XRP but also contributes to the overall growth and adoption of digital assets in the financial world.

Chapter 9: Conclusion

Recap of Key Takeaways

In the exploration of XRP and its implications within the cryptocurrency landscape, several key takeaways emerge that are vital for understanding its significance. First and foremost, XRP is not just a digital currency; it serves a specific purpose in facilitating cross-border payments. Unlike traditional systems that can take days to settle transactions, XRP enables near-instantaneous transfers, drastically reducing the time and cost associated with international money transfers. This efficiency positions XRP as a valuable asset for financial institutions looking to enhance their payment systems.

A comparative analysis of XRP with other cryptocurrencies reveals its unique attributes. While many digital assets operate as speculative investments, XRP is designed with utility in mind. Its consensus mechanism, known as the Ripple Protocol Consensus Algorithm, allows for fast transaction times and scalability, making it distinct from proof-of-work and proof-of-stake mechanisms used by Bitcoin and Ethereum, respectively. This technological advantage reinforces XRP's role as a practical solution for real-world financial needs rather than merely a store of value.

The technology behind XRP, specifically the XRP Ledger, is another focal point that warrants attention. The XRP Ledger is an open-source blockchain that supports not only the transfer of XRP but also the creation of various financial applications. Its decentralized nature ensures security and transparency, while its ability to handle thousands of transactions per second highlights its potential to support a wide array of financial services. Understanding these technological underpinnings is crucial for anyone looking to grasp the full potential of XRP in the evolving digital economy.

XRP's partnerships with financial institutions further underscore its relevance in the contemporary financial ecosystem. Ripple, the company behind XRP, has forged strategic alliances with banks and payment providers around the globe. These collaborations aim to streamline payment processes and enhance the customer experience, showcasing real-world use cases of XRP in action. The growing adoption by established institutions signifies a shift towards modernizing traditional finance, making XRP a key player in this transformation.

Lastly, the relationship between XRP and decentralized finance (DeFi) is an emerging topic that deserves consideration. While DeFi has primarily been associated with Ethereum-based tokens, XRP's unique properties can also contribute to this space. As the DeFi landscape evolves, XRP may find applications in lending, trading, and other financial services, enabling users to leverage its advantages within decentralized frameworks. This intersection not only broadens the scope of XRP's utility but also highlights its potential to adapt and thrive in a rapidly changing financial environment.

The Evolving Landscape of Cryptocurrencies

The cryptocurrency landscape has undergone significant transformation since the inception of Bitcoin in 2009. Initially seen as a niche technology, cryptocurrencies have evolved into a multifaceted ecosystem that encompasses various types of digital assets, each with unique functionalities. This evolution has been driven by technological advancements, regulatory developments, and increasing adoption by both individuals and institutions. As people learning about cryptocurrencies navigate this complex environment, understanding these changes is crucial, particularly for those focusing on XRP and its role in the broader financial system.

XRP, developed by Ripple Labs, is designed primarily for facilitating fast and cost-effective cross-border payments. Unlike traditional cryptocurrencies that often prioritize decentralization, XRP aims to provide a reliable solution for banks and financial institutions seeking to improve their payment systems. This positioning has allowed XRP to carve out a niche within the cryptocurrency market, setting it apart from other digital assets like Bitcoin or Ethereum, which serve different purposes. As XRP's utility in the financial sector becomes more pronounced, it is essential to recognize how this focus has influenced its adoption and market dynamics.

In comparing XRP with other cryptocurrencies, it becomes clear that each asset has its strengths and weaknesses. While Bitcoin is widely regarded as digital gold and Ethereum is celebrated for its smart contract capabilities, XRP's primary advantage lies in its speed and efficiency for cross-border transactions. Transactions using XRP can be settled in seconds, which is a stark contrast to the longer settlement times of traditional banking systems. This unique feature positions XRP as a viable alternative for financial institutions looking to optimize their operations in an increasingly competitive and globalized market.

The technology underlying XRP, particularly the XRP Ledger, plays a crucial role in its functionality. The XRP Ledger is a decentralized blockchain that offers high throughput and low transaction costs, making it suitable for high-volume payment scenarios. In contrast to proof-of-work systems, the XRP Ledger uses a consensus protocol that allows for quick transaction validation. This technological foundation not only enhances the efficiency of XRP but also supports its integration into existing financial infrastructures, making it an attractive option for banks and payment providers looking to leverage blockchain technology.

As decentralized finance (DeFi) continues to gain traction, XRP's role in this evolving landscape remains a topic of discussion. While DeFi primarily focuses on creating financial services without intermediaries, XRP's structured approach aligns well with the needs of regulated financial institutions. Partnerships with banks and payment providers illustrate how XRP can coexist within the DeFi ecosystem, bridging the gap between traditional finance and the emerging world of decentralized applications. As the cryptocurrency landscape evolves, understanding the various roles that assets like XRP play will be essential for anyone looking to navigate this dynamic and rapidly changing field.

Final Thoughts on XRP and Its Potential

XRP presents a unique opportunity within the cryptocurrency landscape, particularly due to its focus on enhancing cross-border payments. As traditional banking systems often struggle with inefficiencies, high fees, and lengthy transaction times, XRP serves as a compelling alternative. Its ability to facilitate near-instantaneous transactions at a fraction of the cost of conventional methods positions it as a pivotal player in the future of global finance. The technology underlying XRP, particularly the XRP Ledger, is designed to provide a secure and scalable solution that can handle high transaction volumes, making it well-suited for institutional use.

When comparing XRP to other cryptocurrencies, it is essential to recognize its distinct advantages and potential drawbacks. While Bitcoin and Ethereum have garnered significant attention and adoption, XRP's specific use case in the financial sector differentiates it. XRP's consensus algorithm allows for faster transaction times and lower energy consumption compared to proof-of-work systems. Furthermore, XRP's partnerships with major financial institutions underscore its commitment to bridging the gap between traditional finance and the burgeoning world of digital assets.

The technology behind XRP, particularly the XRP Ledger, is a testament to its innovative approach. This decentralized platform enables secure, transparent, and efficient transactions, which are essential for financial institutions looking to adopt cryptocurrency solutions. Understanding the technical aspects of XRP can empower users and investors to appreciate its potential fully. The ledger's ability to settle transactions in just a few seconds sets it apart from many other blockchain technologies, which often require longer confirmation times.

XRP's relationships with financial institutions demonstrate its practical applications in real-world scenarios. Ripple, the company behind XRP, has forged partnerships with a multitude of banks and payment providers, enabling them to leverage XRP for enhancing their payment systems. These collaborations not only validate XRP's utility but also reflect a growing recognition of the importance of digital assets in modern finance. As more institutions adopt XRP, its potential for widespread use in cross-border payments becomes increasingly evident.

Finally, considering XRP's place within the decentralized finance (DeFi) ecosystem opens new avenues for its potential growth. While XRP has traditionally been viewed through the lens of cross-border payments, its integration into DeFi platforms suggests that it could play a significant role in lending, borrowing, and liquidity provision. As the DeFi space continues to evolve, XRP's unique attributes may contribute to its adoption and usage beyond merely serving as a bridge currency. The future of XRP is intertwined with the broader developments in cryptocurrency and finance, making it a compelling asset to watch for those interested in the intersection of technology and finance.

www.ingramcontent.com/pod-product-compliance
Lightning Source LLC
LaVergne TN
LVHW081703050326
832903LV00026B/1874